William Huskisson

Pax in bello

A few reflexions on the prospect of peace, arising out of the present

circumstances of the war

William Huskisson

Pax in bello
A few reflexions on the prospect of peace, arising out of the present circumstances of the war

ISBN/EAN: 9783337223915

Hergestellt in Europa, USA, Kanada, Australien, Japan

Cover: Foto ©ninafisch / pixelio.de

Weitere Bücher finden Sie auf **www.hansebooks.com**

PAX IN BELLO;

OR, A

FEW REFLEXIONS

ON THE

PROSPECT of PEACE,

ARISING

OUT of the PRESENT CIRCUMSTANCES

OF THE

WAR.

Juftum et tenacem propofiti Virum,
Non civium ardor prava jubentium,
Non vultus inftantis Tyranni,
Mente quatit folidâ.

LONDON:

Printed for J. OWEN, No. 168, Piccadilly.

1796,

To the READER.

THE following Reflexions were first communicated to the Public through the channel of a Morning Paper.—The object of their Author cannot be mistaken—To support the public Spirit of the Country at this critical Emergency—To avert an ignominious, and to pave the way to an honorable Peace—The probable means of avoiding the one, and securing the other, are discussed without reserve. — Reasons of State may oblige Ministers to confine their Resolutions to the Cabinet—May their result, however, accord with the principles of these Observations! — The Glory of of it will be their own; but an obscure Individual will feel, no less than the greatest Statesman, the glowing exultations of national Honor and public Happiness.

PAX IN BELLO.

THE King's Declarations to Parliament, of his readiness to negotiate with the Enemy, are before the world; and assurances, as unequivocal as satisfactory, have been given by Administration, of their disposition and earnest desire to conclude a *General Peace.*— I shall make these the ground-work of a few observations that have occurred to me, not quite unimportant, perhaps, in the present moment.

Two questions will engage my attention:

First, Is there a disposition in the present Government of France, fairly and *bonâ fide* to meet the avowed wish of this country for a *General Pacification?* Second, On the suppo-

sition

fition that fuch a difpofition exifts, and fhould be manifefted by the French, what are the probabilities of it's being brought to a fpeedy and fatisfactory iffue?

This difcuffion will naturally lead to the terms which the principal Coalefced Powers will expect from France, and the profpect which their fituation and refources, compared to thofe of the enemy, afford of their juft expectations in this refpect being fatisfied.

Many circumftances, arifing in part out of the characters and acknowledged fentiments of the leading men in France, and in part out of the nature and form of their government, induce me to believe that the ideas of thofe who found their hopes of Peace on the moderation and humanity of the enemy will prove illufory; and that the only folid and reafonable grounds of expectation are in the extent of our refources, and in the penurious and exhaufted condition of our adverfary.

Without laying the detail of this confolatory contraft before the public, I truft I fhall find every impartial reader difpofed to admit the general fact; more will not be required to eftablifh tho inferences to be drawn from it.

We

We are anxious for Peace, but when I add, that we are not diftreffed to procure all the means of energetic war, few will be found to contradict my propofition ; and yet perhaps the conviction of it's accuracy arifes from a view of things in fome particulars different from that which led me to this induction.— On the other hand, when I eftimate the means of the Enemy as inadquate to the permanent efforts which the continuance of hoftilities will require from them, I think it will be agreed on all fides, that their expedients are precarious, and not likely to be fuccefsful for any confiderable length of time.—It would be more pleafing to indulge in the hopes of immediate negotiation, and to fee all parties equally inclined to meet on the principles of moderation and equity : — Every obftacle to this moft defirable event muft be traced to the ambition and inadmiffible pretenfions of the French—to them alone will all the calamities which muft attend a prolongation of the War be imputable, if, as I believe, they fhould compel us to forego all expectations of a fpeedy and honorable Peace, except thofe which

which may refult from a vigorous profecution of the War.

Thefe general remarks are drawn from the prefent appearance of affairs, which I fhall endeavour to illuftrate by the language and conduct of the Enemy, and their fituation, compared to that of Great Britain and it's Allies. It never was of greater importance that they fhould be fully known to the Public, who, over-fanguine, from mifapprehenfion of the King's Meffage, have lately formed expectations, not warranted by circumftances. Thefe expectations would lead to difappointment, and difappointment to defpondency, and pufillanimous conceffion, if not properly counteracted. Minifters fhould be much on their guard, that their meaning is not thus miftaken, if, as I am perfuaded, they are really anxious to obtain a good and honorable Peace. Without being acquainted with their plans, I certainly fhare this fentiment; and, urged by it's impulfe, I will communicate my opinions, unreftrained by any other confideration than thofe which muft actuate every Englifhman, when the dignity and welfare of his country are at ftake.

I have

I have already expreffed my apprehenfions, that there does not exift, on the part of the Enemy, a difpofition to treat for a General Peace, in the manner pointed out in His Majefty's Meffage.

Nothing can, however, be more diftant from my intentions, than to infinuate that the French Government does not forcibly feel all the difficulties and embarraffments of War, and a proportionate anxiety for its termination. Whatever defcription of men may now be at the head of affairs in France, it is impoffible to fuppofe, that they fhould not more or lefs conne&t the continuance of their power, and the permanency and ftability of their arrangements, with the ceffation of thofe violent and convulfive efforts, by which fupplies are procured.

The influence of this confideration, in the decifions of France, depends on the views and fentiments of the exifting Government.

The perfons who oppofed the forced re-ele&tion of two-thirds of the Convention, and were well-wifhers to the Se&tions of *Paris* in their late glorious ftruggle, form what I fhall call *the Moderate Party*. Crufhed on the
5th

5th and 6th of October laft, its leading Members have been excluded from the Councils of the Republic, and from all participation in the Executive Directory; but it is not ufelefs here to recal their opinions on the great queftion of Peace and War, inasmuch as they will throw a confiderable light on thofe of their fuccefsful adverfaries. They were convinced that the reftitution of their conquefts was indifpenfably neceffary to the fpeedy return of Peace; that this reftitution would be attended with no difgrace, provided the Liberty and independence of the French Republic were acknowledged by the Coalefced Powers. This laft point they confidered as the object of the War; and the accomplifhment of that object as the criterion of a fecure and honourable Peace.—If this Party had been more fortunate, an event fo very defirable might now have been in a train of Negotiation.

What, on the other hand, are the avowed fentiments of the prevailing Faction? A determination to keep their conquefts; and, for this end, wickedly to perfevere in the War, under the expectation, that the preffure of it's calamities will foon be fo feverely felt by the
Combined

Combined Powers, as to force them to confirm, by a Treaty, this monſtrous aggrandizement of their Republic.—Every ſtep of
the preſent Government has evinced their re-
ſolution not to depart from this Syſtem. The
well-diſpoſed People of France, knowing this
to be their determination, appear no longer
to indulge in the proſpect of a ſpeedy Pacification. They are not ignorant of our reſources, and muſt be ſenſible, that an abſolute
inability to continue the conteſt, can alone induce us to ſubmit to ſuch Terms. The natural
inference to be drawn from this ſtate of things
(liable, however, to many modifications, but
certainly fully applicable to the preſent poſture
of affairs,) is, that the War muſt be carried
on till one of the contending Parties has con-
ſumed every adequate means of continuing it,
and then, that the ruined Power muſt receive
the terms which the other may be pleaſed to
dictate. Both are wearied and anxious to give
over, but not exhauſted. The charge of cri-
minal ambition reſts ſolely with our Enemy;
and I heſitate not to predict, that it will end
in their complete diſappointment. In vain the
Directory will have recourſe to the plunder of
private

private Property, and to every odious expedient of the System of Terror. The full proof of the insufficiency of these means may be found in their own official statements.—Do they suppose we can be duped and misled by the arrogant and menacing language in which these humiliating avowals of their weakness are conveyed to the Public? Is Austria to be terrified into a degrading Treaty by their haughty and indecent behaviour to Count *Carletti?* In vain do they attempt to stigmatize the Advocates for Peace and Moderation by the name of *La Faction des Anciens Limites.* These unfortunate friends to their country are become the objects of their persecution. Do they expect, by this barbarous policy, to convince and overawe Europe? Convinced we may be of their pertinacious adherence to their absurd and inadmissible schemes, but indignation, and not fear, spirited unanimity and perseverance, and not shameful despondency and submission, will be the result of that conviction. Europe may learn, by several recent diplomatic appointments, the determination of the Directory to place their future Negotiations in the hands of pure *Jacobins,* resolved to listen to no

alternative,

alternative, *but Peace on their own terms, or War*. But Europe may refuse to treat with such *Jacobins*; and I hope soon to satisfy every unprejudiced person, that such will naturally be the conduct of the Allies, until France shall have departed from her lofty and preposterous pretensions, of which every intimation is an insult to Two great Powers, who have firmly resolved to make a joint and honourable Peace their common object.—The one, Master of the Sea, having reduced under it's dominion the most important Colonies in the World, possessed of immense pecuniary resources:— The other, victorious on the *Rhine*, and diligently providing it's numerous Armies with every means of improving their brilliant and rapid successes.—Both just and moderate in their views, united in their efforts, and rivals only in ardour and emulation. Who can doubt that they will remain inseparable in this glorious pursuit, until they shall have compelled the Enemy to sue for terms, consistent with the dignity of their Crowns, the lasting interests and security of their possessions, and the permanent tranquillity of Europe?

C   The

The late communications from *Paris* have confirmed the apprehenfions I entertained of the difpofition of the French Government with refpect to the King's Meffage.

The infulting language of the Papers under the influence of the Directory, accords very ill with any profpects of Peace; and the principal ufe made by their injured adverfaries, of the little Liberty of the Prefs which ftill remains in France, is, to lament the inevitable continuance of the War, and the certain mifery and calamities which it muft bring on their devoted Country.—" To re-create our Navy, to recruit " our Armies, to find fupplies for at leaft " another Campaign, are the objects (fays one " of their Papers) which muft now engage " our attention."—A difficult, if not an impracticable undertaking! Let us recollect, that our Navy flourifhes beyond all former example; that the Auftrian Battalions are not mouldered away by defertion, or inefficient from want of recruits; that our Supplies for the year are provided; that pecuniary aid can be furnifhed to our Ally, without embarraffment, or diminution of credit: and having thus compared thefe our relative fituations, let

us

us have a proper fenfe of the immenfe fuperiority of our own refources, and feel, as we
ought to do, the overbearing infolence of an
Enemy, pretending to dictate terms, to which,
though as much reduced as themfelves, it
would be infamy to liften, and ruin to fubmit.

If the Plans of the French Government may
be judged of by their official proceedings, they
correfpond fo exactly to my conception and
ftatement of their intentions, that I cannot help
noticing them on this occafion : — *Another
Campaign, brilliant and decifive, or Peace on our
own terms.* — Such is the fubftance of their
Letter to the Minifter of War, on the fufpen-
fion of arms, which a laudable defire to avoid
the bloody fkirmifhing, and harraffing fatigue
of Patrules and Out-pofts, appears to have dictated to the Generals on the *Rhine*, on fending
the hoftile Armies into Winter-quarters. I
give them full credit for their candid and
obliging affurance, that they are willing to
grant Peace to Europe on their own terms;
but I fee little reafon to apprehend that they
are efficiently prepared for the other alternative,
on which, however, they appear firmly refolved; modeftly condefcending to inform us, at

the

the fame time, that it is not their intention to require " Terms deftructive of the fafety of " other Powers, but fuch only as are confift- " ent with the intereft of thofe Powers *well* " *underftood*."—If any one is at a lofs to know what thefe Gentlemen mean by the interefts of Europe *well underftood*; they may find an explanation in the Minifter *Merlin's* Report for annexing the Netherlands to France, in which he ingenuoufly afferts, that Nature has affigned the *Rhine* for the Boundary of the Re- public, and *Paris* for its Capital, as being, by this extenfion of it's limits, nearly in a centri- cal pofition ; and if he fhould not be fatisfied by this very *natural* logic of the firft Chancel- lor of the new Republic, let him read *Carnot's* opinion on the fame fubject, who more honeftly and plainly proves, that, by uniting the Nether- lands to France, her refiftance would be ren- dered for' ever fecure, and her attacks irrefift- ible.

The joint eloquence of the Lawyer and the Soldier carried the Decree of Re-union, and as a reward for their exertions, the one is placed in the Miniftry, and the other fits in the Di- rectory, with four other Colleagues; no lefs

ftrenuous

ftrenuous than himfelf in their fupport of this very *natural* meafure; but *natural and well-underflood* as it may appear to them, it will require at leaft all the arguments of a *very brilliant Campaign*, to convince the Powers of Europe, that they ought, on this occafion, to make thefe enlightened and impartial Sovereigns the arbiters of their refpective interefts, without prefuming to think or reafon for themfelves.

I fhall not dwell any longer on the avowed hoftile difpofition of the Enemy; but, as fooner or later they muft either make or receive overtures of Peace, it becomes interefting to endeavour to collect, from their opinions and conduct, in what manner they would probably proceed under each of thefe contingencies.

Should the firft fteps towards Negotiation be made by the French, it muft be evident to every obferver of events, that they will endeavour, by all poffible expedients, to difunite the Allies, and by negotiating with them feparately, to attain, in the partial advantages of each unconnected Treaty, a refult conformable to the Plan they have chalked out for a general Pacification.

On

On the other hand, the engagements of this Country, and the interest of Europe, require of the Administration to refuse all overtures which have not for their object a General Peace. With an interest at stake infinitely greater, the Emperor is bound by the same engagements, and would, I am perfuaded, equally with ourfelves, reject all infidious propofals for partial Negotiation.

This difficulty, I have always confidered as the greateft obftacle to the commencement of Negotiation.

From the temper of the French Government, I am afraid, it will continue to impede this defirable event, after feveral others fhall have been removed. It is for want of a fufficient confideration of the diftinct and different interefts of the contending Parties in a point fo very material, and of their oppofite conduct and declarations, founded on this effential difference, that the expectations of Peace, which were the firft refult of the King's Meffage, appear to me to have been fo much over-rated, in the opinion of the Public of this Country, and of Europe.

Some

Some were induced to hope and believe that a Negotiation was actually in train—Others, that some explanation had been had with the Enemy, who had required this oftensible declaration as a preliminary to an amicable arrangement already agreed upon.—All were of opinion, that the Message, as relating to a *General Peace*, had been concerted with our Allies, and made public with their concurrence; and no one had the least doubt that it had effectually removed the chief, if not the only obstacle to an immediate Peace.

Instead of these pleasing illusions, the truth is, that the King, by stating that the nature of the present Government would no longer be an insurmountable bar to all Negotiation, has certainly rendered it practicable, as soon as either Party shall determine to have recourse to this desirable measure; but the numerous difficulties by which it might be retarded or prevented, remain in their full force, and have been considerably augmented by the conduct of France since the Message was delivered.

It is so far from my intention to undervalue the true importance of this Message, that I have no hesitation to say, that if the *Moderate Party*

Party had prevailed, His Majefty's pacific Intentions would have been joyfully met by fimilar intentions on their part; and this happy difpofition on both fides might, by this period, have had it's full and falutary effect; for their principles and views would have coincided with the wifhes and juft expectations of Europe. By the prefent Party, the Meffage has probably been received with great concern, inafmuch as it muft attach to them alone, in the confideration of the fuffering People of France, and in the opinion of every Englifhman, the charge of the prolongation of the War, and thereby, on the one hand, weaken their authority, and, on the other, give to our efforts additional union and energy.

Mr. Pitt's Declaration in Parliament, that the Meffage was not in contemplation when he contracted for the Loan, is a proof that our Allies had not been confulted on the occafion, and confequently Adminiftration could not be prepared to make, or anfwer any fpecific propofals for a general Pacification, which, if they fhould originate with us, muft necefarily be previoufly confidered and concerted with our Allies; and for the fame reafon, if

coming

coming from our Enemy, can only be received as a communication on which the opinions of the Allies would be taken. Since the delivery of the Meſſage, I know no difference between the principle of the preſent and any former War with France; which I conſider as the only real change it has effected.

How long this approach towards a Pacification may be counteracted by the preſent Rulers of France, I cannot pretend to ſay; but they are ſo committed by their unwary and violent proceedings, that any favourable change of meaſures muſt be the effect of compulſion alone, and will probably be the reſult of a failure in their reſources—.Under the preſent circumſtances, I ſee no other reaſonable chance of Peace.

The Directory and the Majority of both the Councils of the Republic have acquired power by flattering the paſſions of the Mob and the Army, and courting their applauſe and ſupport, in oppoſition to the Landed and Monied Intereſt of the Empire; and, unfortunately, with theſe inſtruments, they have, in every inſtance, met with ſucceſs—But the conſequence is, that they ſtand pledged to their

D   friends,

friends, and bound by their opinions and paſt conduct, to be governed and directed by the ſame doctrines; and from habit, inclination, or the pride of appearing conſiſtent, they ſtill court the applauſe and good-will of the Populace, inflame their paſſions, and particularly that zeal for aggrandizement, plunder, and falſe glory, which is ſo eaſily grafted on an Army long victorious, and ſtill more eaſily diffuſed through a People agitated by enthuſiaſm, and all the viciſſitudes and torments of a Revolution.

A deluded Populace, who has nothing at ſtake, cares not if the whole Property of the Country is ſacrificed to a miſtaken principle of National Honour.

The glory of extending the Republic to the *Rhine*, is the boon of every *Jacobin*, who, truſting to the ſpirited perſeverance of his friends in the Directory, enjoys daily his ſhare of their imaginary triumph.

This obſtacle to a reſtitution of their Conqueſts, the *ſine qua non* of Peace, inherent to the form and nature of their Government, is no ſmall addition to the difficulties of a General Pacification.

In

In the prefent fituation of affairs, and with the difpofition manifefted by the Enemy, it appears impoffible to indulge in the hope of a fpeedy Negotiation, and confequently it becomes our intereft and our duty once more to rally round the Standard of War, not with a view of preferving ourfelves from the contagion of Revolutionary Principles, nor to prevent or affift in the eftablifhment of any particular Government in France, but to oblige her to reftore her conquefts, and to return within her former limits.

This is a juft, irrefiftible, and preffing motive for the continuance of hoftilities. That the Netherlands fhould be recovered, that Holland fhould not be in the direct dependence, and under the immediate controul of France, are conditions indifpenfible to the fafety and commercial interefts of this Country; to the repofe of Europe, which would otherwife be at the mercy of an overgrown Republic, governed by Jacobins, and (what would be ftill more alarming) actuated by the fpirit of conqueft. The examples of Confifcation and Plunder, the contagion of Revolutionary Doctrines, the fanaticifm of the Rights

of

of Man, once appeared an almost irresistible torrent, destroying, in it's rapid progress, all social distinctions, and every advantage derived from property and civilization. It's course has been stopped by energy and perseverance. Let us act with the same spirit in the present instance, and the Barriers which guard the Balance of Power, and the Political Independence of the North of Europe, will ultimately be replaced in their former positions; and though there is reason to apprehend that we are at some distance from the attainment of this point, and that it must be carried *sword in hand*, the consideration of the terms which this Country and it's Allies might expect, and ought to require, on the supposition of an immediate Negotiation, is certainly an interesting subject of investigation.

The conditions to be procured for our Allies on the Continent will form the first part of our enquiry, and may be discussed separately from the terms which relate to Colonies and distant Possessions, in which England is more immediately concerned.

It cannot be denied, that a general anxiety for Peace prevails in this and every other Country

Country engaged in the conteft againft France; that it is much increafed by the prefent fcarcity of provifions, and by the daily preffure of the accumulated calamities, infeparable from a ftate of War.

Under thefe circumftances, it is the duty of the feveral Powers to concur in the wifhes of their Subjects, and to reftore them to the bleffings of Peace, as foon as it can be effected, without the facrifice of the honour and permanent interefts of their refpective States : But it is a duty, no lefs effential to the character of a Statefman, more arduous to fulfil without indifcretion, and rendered infinitely more requifite by the temper of the Enemy, to refift, in a firm and prudent manner, the interefted clamours of Party, and the obftreperous impatience of the inconfiderate Multitude.— The momentary lofs of popularity is attended with too many unpleafant confequences to be an object of indifference to any Minifter; but if he be upright, and equal to the difficulties of his fituation, he will never put it in competition with a fteady adherence to the line of conduct he will neceffarily trace out for himfelf on every great occafion, and in this

he

he will be guided by his own judgment, aided and directed by a fenfe of duty, and of the importance of the truft repofed in him.

I freely own, that the opinion I entertain of the Adminiftration of this Country, and of the Cabinet of Vienna, is not inferior to my conception of their tafk in this refpect; and with a full confidence that it will be well and faithfully performed, I have no hefitation to fay, that it cannot be fo, and that they will juftly forfeit every claim to gratitude and efteem, if the unlimited reftitution of all the principal Conquefts of France in Europe be not made the leading feature and invariable principle of all Negotiation relative to the Pacification of the Continent.

I do not wifh to be underftood, that we muft require the ftrict *Status quo ante Bellum*, becaufe I fhould lament to fee the War protracted for the poffeffion of a paltry Village, or a few miferable acres on the Frontier, which, from particular fituation, or other circumftances, might peculiarly affect the interefts, or fuit the convenience of either party; but France cannot be allowed to retain any confiderable territorial Conqueft of great extent,

produce,

produce, and population, important by it's refources, and infinitely more fo by it's fituation
with refpect to commercial advantages, and
military and naval power. Such are the Netherlands, and the contiguous Countries and
Fortreffes which have been annexed to the
French Republic. Their vaft confequence in
the Balance of Power, confidered under each
of thefe heads, is fo forcibly felt by all the
Northern States of Europe, and has been the
foundation and origin of fo many Alliances,
Difputes, Wars, and Treaties, that it cannot
be neceffary to dwell long on a fubject, which
makes fo confpicuous a part of Modern Hiftory, and in which the Maritime and Commercial Powers (and England in particular)
will almoft always be found to have taken a
leading and principal concern.

An impartial appeal to the uniform conduct
of our Anceftors, will convince every unprejudiced man of the importance of the object
at ftake —Any detailed illuftration of this
great Political Truth, is an undertaking to
which I am unequal, and, moreover, too ex-
tenfive for the prefent occafion; I fhall therefore confine myfelf to a few obfervations, to
prove

prove that the motives which rendered the Netherlands fo principal an object in War and Peace, and of fo much weight in all former Treaties, are fully applicable to the prefent fituation of affairs, and particularly with a reference to the interefts of this Country.

The Netherlands, and the conquered Countries annexed to the French Republic, by the Decree of the Convention of the 1ft of October, 1795, may be confidered either as fubfervient to Power, or as conducive to the purpofes and advantages of Navigation and Commerce.

France, from it's pofition, compactnefs, and feveral other natural advantages, aided and ameliorated by it's fortifications, and the numerous improvements of art, was poffeffed, even within the confines of it's former limits, of a preponderance, as a Military Power, in the balance of Europe, which, for more than a century, it has been very difficult effectually to oppofe and counteract—an object in which the other great Continental Powers muft certainly have failed, in fome former War, if they had not been, from time to time, fupported by the pecuniary refources of this Country and of Holland. Every well-wifher to the permanent tranquillity of Europe must regret, that this support, and all the exertions which it has occasionally called forth, have not completely prevented the aggrandizement of the French Empire, since the Peace of *Utrecht*. It's acquisitions, however, though far from unimportant, are not to be compared with it's present pretensions, rendered, by the accession of strength derived from these same acquisitions, and by the present relative situations of France and Holland, infinitely more inadmissible, than at any of the former periods in which they have been opposed by this Country.

It would be an useless repetition of facts, known to every man not totally unacquainted with the history of Flanders, to state, that it abounds in all the productions, and possesses every advantage, which contribute to the wealth and prosperity of a Country in time of Peace, and to its resources and vigour in time of War —fertility of soil, population, manufactures, commerce, industry, public establishments, fortifications, and positions invaluable either for attack or defence, rivers, and facilities for communication, and every other purpose mili-

tary

tary and commercial.—Thefe, and many other advantages equally important, and incalculable in their confequences, would be placed at the difpofal of France, by any Treaty which left her in poffeffion of the conquered Countries, and of the fortreffes ceded by the Dutch, by their late Treaty with that Power. Thefe ceffions, which include Maeftricht, Venloo, Dutch Flanders, and the right fide of the Hondt, were certainly neceffary to the permanent fecurity of their conquefts, and were evidently required, with a view to the completion of that plan of aggrandizement, to which they vainly expect the Belligerent Powers will be compelled to fubmit. Mafters, by their difmemberment of Holland, of the mouth of the Scheldt, they are thereby poffeffed of an excellent and fecure harbour at the extremity of the Channel oppofite to the Thames, and fuperior to every other fituation for the protection or annoyance of Trade in the Downs, or in the North Seas. In Maeftricht and Venloo they have the keys of Holland, and the undifturbed poffeffion of the Meufe; and even if thefe two fortreffes were reftored to the Dutch, as long as the French fhould retain Flanders, they

would

would still be in their immediate dependence;
and, by this dependence, the refources of the
United Provinces would remain, as they now
are, entirely at the difpofal of France. It will
not require much political fagacity, to eftimate
the effects of their *proconfular* afcendancy over
the Government of the United Provinces, combined with their *fovereign* authority over all
the Emperor's poffeffions on the left banks of
the Rhine; although fome of the inevitable
confequences might be more or lefs retarded
by the peculiar circumftances in which France
will probably find herfelf at the concluíion of
a Peace; and particularly thofe which would,
neverthelefs, in a fhort time, moft materially
and fatally affect the Commercial Intercourfe
and Maritime Power of this Kingdom. Motives of policy, intereft, or neceffity, founded
on the annihilation of trade and capitals in
France, or other very urgent grounds, may
induce them to fuffer us to trade with the
Ports of Holland and Flanders for a few years;
but that intercourfe muft depend entirely, as
to its nature, extent and duration, on their
good will and pleafure; muft be tributary to
their power and government, and will be

hampered

hampered by such arbitrary restrictions, as they will gradually impose, until they can exclude us from it altogether. We should then be deprived of our beneficial and extensive Commerce with Flanders, the greatest part of Germany, and the North of Europe, and confined in our connexions with those parts of the world, to a precarious intercourse with the Ports of the Weser and the Elbe, or Ports still less conveniently situated—Competition with the French and Dutch would be found impossible—They would become not only the carriers of the productions we might have to dispose of, but the regulators of the market in which they would be sold.

Let those, who, from presumption and ignorance, tell the People of this Country that we ought not to interfere, or take any concern in the affairs of the Continent, meditate on these great truths, and the inevitable consequences, to which the adoption of their errors would infallibly lead. Whenever this pernicious doctrine is presented to the Public, by men possessed of great talents, brilliantly employed in the investigation and discussion of the public concerns of their Country and of Europe, I am more disposed to

to fufpect their fincerity than their underftanding; and the regret I feel, that a fpirit of Party,
or the purfuit of Popularity, fhould induce
them to impede the attainment of points which
no Adminiftration can relinquifh, is mixed
with a juft indignation, arifing from the en-
couragement they thereby afford the Enemy
to perfevere in their pretenfions.—I hefitate not
to declare, that there is no Party in this Kingdom, which, in power, would dare to propofe
Peace with France on the terms in queftion;
and I challenge thofe who affect to afcribe the
continuance of the War to the ambitious and
hoftile views of the prefent Adminiftration, to
deny the affertion.

The unfortunate effects which would arife
from the precarious dependence of fo precious
and confiderable a proportion of our European
Trade on the will of the French and Dutch,
and its confequent gradual decay, would foon
be felt in the diminution of our credit, our
refources, and of our weight and influence on
the Continent, and in the affairs of *Europe*.

Thefe calamities, inevitable from the nature
of things, under the fuppofition of the Ceffion of
the *Netherlands*, would foon be followed by an
innumerable

innumerable train of national misfortunes, proportioned in their magnitude to the prefent immenfe extent of our interior and external Trade, our Manufactures, Induftry, and Refources of every defcription—All thefe advantages afford a mutual fupport to each other, and on the fupport and prefervation of the whole depend the ftability of our Credit, and the folidity of our Public Debt.

If we enquired into the firft great, and, I truft, durable fource of our flourifhing condition, every true Englifhman will trace it to the *Conftitution*; but under it, our prefent profperity is the refult of the happy accord, juft proportion, and relative influence and extenfion of all the abovementioned caufes, feconded and improved by judicious regulations, aided by fagacious arrangements, enterprifing fpeculations, ingenious improvements, and that public fpirit, which, in every part of the world, is confidered as the honourable characteriftic of the induftrious and commercial part of the Britifh Community. The political and commercial Exiftence of this Country may be compared to the working of a ftupendous and complicated machine, aftonifhing the fpectators

by

by the harmony and regularity of its ftructure, the correctnefs of its movements, the juft and admirable proportion between its effects and the caufes by which they are produced; but fo delicate in its interior parts, that none can be materially altered, fufpended, or withdrawn, without deranging and ultimately deftroying thefe happy refults. In fuch a machine, how many efficient fprings, important to the prefervation of the whole, may efcape the common obferver's eye, which are, at the fame time, objects of unremitting care and attention to its well-informed, judicious, and upright Directors?

The importance to this Country of not fuffering *Flanders* and *Holland* to remain in the hands or dependence of the French, is, I hope, fatisfactorily eftablifhed in the opinion of every impartial man.

Paffion, Prejudice, or a rafh defire to ftipulate for an immediate Peace, may have led fome to a different conclufion. Should their intentions be honeft, thefe obfervations may perhaps induce them to reconfider the fubject. But if they are the blind flaves of Faction; the devoted and irretrievable Zealots of French Syftems;

or

[32]

or pufillanimous Egotifts, coldly facrificing the
future grandeur and interefts of their Country
to momentary and infecure repofe; adhering
to their opinions, let them triumph in the expectation of retarding an honourable arrangement, by every obftacle and impediment which
can raife the hopes of the Enemy, or thwart
the juft purfuits of Government.—Let them
triumph in the infatuated delufion, that this
extenfion of French Power will give countenance and fupport to Revolutionary Doctrines;
pave the way to the fubverfion of all diftinc-
tions of Rank and Property; and, finally, lead
to the great object of their purfuits—the deftruction of *Monarchy* and *Chriftianity*, and the
divifion of *Europe* into Republics founded on
the *Rights of Man*.—Let them triumph in their
ignominious difregard of Public Faith and National Honor; in their profligate indifference
to the deareft interefts of Pofterity; and in the
contemptible gratification of thofe felfish paf-
fions, which they bafely prefer to the generous
dictates of Public Spirit. Thefe triumphs
fhall be exclufively their own—unenvied by all
who cannot fhare them, and abhorred by every
Englifhman, who wifhes, with confiftent judg-

ment

ment and manly pride, to walk in the paths
of his Anceftors, and to look forward, as they
did, to provide for the happinefs of future
generations.

The grounds on which I have hitherto con-
tended againft the aggrandizement of *France*,
form but an inconfiderable part of the motives
for ftrenuoufly refifting every propofal to that
effect. Moft of the arguments I have adduced,
are taken from commercial confiderations, and
applicable only to the ftate of peace and of
good underftanding between *France* and *England*.—However ferious the profpect may appear, under this contingency, it will be found
infinitely more alarming, if we look forward
to the renewal of hoftilities. The French and
Dutch would be ftudioufly employed, during
the interval of Peace, in diftreffing our Commerce, and proportionally extending their
own—in re-eftablifhing and increafing their Naval Force—in completing and improving their
new Harbours oppofite to the Britifh Coafts—
in cementing their Union fo as to combine
their efforts, and render their joint exertions
as efficient as if they were directed by one Government. Moft great coalitions have failed,
becaufe the principal ends for which they were

F

formed,

formed, have been facrificed by fome of their Members to their petty jealoufies, fecret views, or feparate interefts; but in the prefent cafe there would exift a ftrict unity both of Power and Intereft.—Of Power, becaufe the *French* Government has a fupreme afcendency over that of *Holland*—Of Intereft, becaufe, as long as the Councils of the *United Provinces* fhall be governed by *France*, it will be their firft object, as Maritime and Commercial Powers, to deprive *England* of its Naval Superiority. Unequal as they now appear, in any refpect, to contend with us for the Empire of the Sea, it would appear, by a late Meffage of the Executive Directory, that, in their wild prefumption, they entertain hopes of not terminating the prefent War, until they fhall have avenged their difafters at *Toulon*, the defeats of the 1ft of June, 1794, and the 23d of June, 1795.—Let any *Englifhman* take up the abovementioned Meffage, and read in it—

" *That every effort fhall be made to fit out Squadrons, competent to meet and conquer their cruel and implacable Enemy, whofe perfidious Politics juftify their hatred, and call for exemplary vengeance.—That this is the object of all their hopes—the end of all their efforts—the cry heard*

from

from every part of the Republic. That it is by accomplishing this object that they will procure for France a Peace, such as they have a right to expect, founded on the defeat and humiliation of their Maritime Rival." * He is unworthy of his Country, if it does not excite in him the strongest feelings of contempt and indignation; for it never can be congenial to the British Character to be terrified into submission by this pitiful outrage, which will lead us to shew our resentment, not by a vain imitation of the insignificant menaces of our Enemy, but by a steady resolution never to depart from our just pretensions, and chearfully to bear such farther sacrifices as may be necessary, finally to subdue the perverse and uncontrouled ambition of the French Republic.— Any immediate expectation of meeting us at sea appears so preposterous, that I can only attribute their language, in this respect, to an unguarded indulgence of a passion, which, on too many occasions, has influenced their Councils—I mean a decided enmity to this Country, apportioned to the vigorous and noble

F 2 efforts,

* See the Message of the Directory to the Council of Five Hundred, on the necessity of re-establishing their Navy.

efforts, by which we have fucceffively oppofed their fchemes of Revolution and Aggrandizement.

: If, by the refult of a General Pacification, they could retain their Influence 'in *Holland*, and obtain the ceffion of the *Netherlands*, I am convinced that, with thefe terms, they would be graciously pleafed to adjourn the execution of their plan for *humbling their Maritime Rival* until the firft renewal of hoftilities.

. . The interval, from the conclufion of a Peace to that period, would, probably, be fhort, but long enough to enable them to turn to effect the advantages of a Treaty, which would fo materially increafe the means of improving their Maritime Power. Their extent of coaft, oppofite to the Britifh fhore, would, in that cafe, reach from *Breft* to the *Texel*, of which all the important harbours, between *Dunkirk* and the laft mentioned port, would have been acquired fince the commencement of the War; in addition to a confiderable number of fecondary ports, advantageoufly fituated for fitting out and fheltering Privateers ; and for the annoyance of our Trade, they would poffefs, in the *German* and *North Seas*, not only the *Texel* but *Fluffing*,

Flufhing, and other valuable harbours formed by the *Scheldt*; and if to thefe two principal ports they fhould add *Cherbourg*, which it would then be fo much their intereft to complete, this line would be rendered moft formidable either for attack or defence. It would include four chief ports, all at a very fmall diftance from *England*, and fo apportioned in their refpective diftances from each other, as to give folidity and fupport to the whole line, and to afford, at the fame time, the utmoft facility for communication, for collecting their force and combining their operations, and for retreat, in cafe of defeat or fuperiority of numbers. It will be eafy to draw to thefe Ports, and particularly to the two fituated on the *German Sea*, every means of rapidly eftablifhing a Naval Power. The forefts of the conquered Countries, their eafy intercourfe with the North, the nautical difpofition of the *Dutch* and *Flemings*, and the extenfion of trade, would foon furnifh them with every requifite for a powerful Navy. It may be objected that, although *Holland* and the *Netherlands* have been for fome time, and ftill continue, fubject to the French Government, none of the inconveniencies

veniencies fo much apprehended have been
experienced by this Country. This objection
will have no weight with thofe who have
carefully attended to the events of the prefent
War, but for the many who have not, it is
neceffary that it fhould be properly inveftigated,
and anfwered; and this confideration will
naturally lead to an inquiry into the importance of the *Netherlands*, as the great bond of
union between this Country and the Powers at
prefent our Allies, or with which we may hereafter have to co-operate againft the ambitious
views of *France*; and before we take leave of
the fuppofition, that the *Low Countries* will be
ceded to *France*, it will not be foreign to our
fubject to ftate, what, under that contingency,
might be our fituation, in cafe of a renewal
of hoftilities. This event ought to be guarded
againft; but is too probable to be overlooked
in a Treaty of Peace, and may take place
between *France* and *England*, unfupported by
any Ally, or we may act in conjunction with
fome of the principal Continental Powers.
An impartial difcuffion of either of thefe circumftances, I am convinced, will only tend to
eftablifh and confirm our former conclufions.

Some

Some of the reasons which have prevented the French from deriving any great maritime advantages from *Flanders* and *Holland*, during the present War, are so obvious, that they must occur to every one on the first consideration of the subject. When Flanders was captured, they had three Naval Powers to contend with, and Armies to maintain, vastly superior in numbers to those of all the Powers engaged in the Coalition. Assuredly the last of these contingencies was sufficient to require all the resources of Flanders, which, it must also be observed, could not have been applied with effect to naval objects, until the French were assisted, instead of being counteracted, by Holland. When the United Provinces fell into their hands, they had still to oppose the same pressure from the Continental Powers, and the enormous contributions they levied were applied to the support of their Armies.

The War, moreover, had then been carried on with vigour for two years; and during these two years, by our unparalleled exertions to augment our Naval Forces, and by a series of successful attacks on those of the French, we had acquired, in this respect, such a decided superiority,

periority, as could not have been eafily wrefted from us by the Enemy, even if they had not been under the neceffity of appropriating to the fervice of their Armies the additional means and refources procured in Holland.

On their firft taking poffeffion of the United Provinces, they were, I fuppofe, not unaware of thefe circumftances, and were probably little at liberty to choofe between the uncertain and diftant project of naval enterprife, and the immediate preffing wants of a victorious and exacting Army. If we revert to the events of laft year, to the further deftruction and difperfion of their Squadrons, to the great augmentation of Britifh Ships in Commiffion, to the fuccefs of the new expedient for manning them adopted by Parliament, and to the affiftance afforded by the co-operation of the Ruffian Fleet, we fhall be convinced, that the Enemy's determination to make their Maritime Power a fecondary confideration, was pointed out to them, by the relative circumftances of the two Countries, as the only policy they could purfue at that period of the War.

Europe has witneffed, with aftonifhment, the efforts of French Tyranny under their

new

new form of Government, and the celerity with which it has enabled them to execute the moſt gigantic plans. At the commencement of a future rupture, the ſame deſpotic authority may ſtill prevail, and may again have re-courſe to expedients equally violent and irre-ſiſtible. If it ſhould be a War between France and England alone, (a circumſtance by no means improbable, in the ſuppoſition of the ceſſion of Holland and the Netherlands) the former, diſentangled from all her embarraſsments, might then turn it's whole attention to the ſpeedy equipment of a powerful Navy.—For this purpoſe, their acquiſitions of Coaſt and Territory would certainly afford them every requiſite means of executing the moſt exten- ſive projects which ambition, and a deſire to avenge ſo many late defeats at Sea, can ſuggeſt to an active, enterprizing, and reſtleſs Government, conſcious of the uncontrouled magnitude of it's power, and elated by it's exten- ſive conqueſts.—Whatever glory theſe con-queſts may reflect on their victorious Armies muſt be tarniſhed by the humiliations of their ſcattered and vanquiſhed Fleets.

This is a juft fubject of pride and confolation to England ; but prudence and experience
forbid us to indulge in the expectation, that
the fpirit of a haughty and refentful Rival
will be fubdued by the mortifying contraft.
On the contrary, it would roufe their hatred,.
and urge them to feize the firft opportunity of
turning againft us the advantages pufillani-
moufly left at their difpofal. We fhould then
have tenfold reafon to deprecate the truth of
an obfervation, of which we have too often
felt the weight in former Wars, where we had
only to oppofe progreffive and regular operations, directed by the feeble and contracted
power of the old Government, confined to it's
own refources, and to the limits of the Monarchy. The obfervation to which I allude is,
that at the breaking out of a War, the French
are in general better prepared for it, and more
expeditious than we are, in bringing forward
their Forces. If France fhould find it practicable to equip and fend to fea, in the firft
fix months of any future War, a Naval Force
equal to what every exertion of this Country
could provide in double the time, our moft
valuable trade would probably fall into their
hands—

hands—With our trade we fhould lofe our
Seamen, on whofe return our chief dependence
for refiftance and fuccefs muft reft, whenever
this Country is involved in hoftilities.—France
was placed in a fimilar fituation by our numerous captures at the commencement of the
feven years War—It's effects were not recovered
during the whole of that conteft, and ultimately led to the deftruction of her Navy, and
the confequent lofs of many valuable Colonies,
which procured to this Country the glorious
Peace of 1763—The recollection of that Peace
ftill rankles in the mind of every Frenchman.
Shall the noble fpirit by which it was dictated
ceafe to excite our emulation, while it remains
an object of inveterate refentment to the Enemy, exafperated too by the Naval Triumphs
and Colonial Conquefts of the prefent War?

With refpect to our Colonies, if we were
not prepared to meet the French at fea, their
expeditions might then proceed againft them,
with the certainty of not being intercepted on
their paffage, or molefted in their operations;
and it would require but a very inconfiderable
proportion of the Land Forces, conftantly at
their difpofal, to wreft our moft valuable diftant

poffeffions

poſſeſſions from the weak Garriſons by which
they are defended on the Peace Eſtabliſhment.—
In leſs than one Campaign, all this might be
effected, and ſuch means of defence eſtabliſhed
for their preſervation, as would render every
futu:e attempt to retake them abortive, ſhould
the French once acquire and maintain (though
for a ſhort period) that Naval ſuperiority, which,
in Peace or War, it muſt be our conſtant aim
to prevent.

Should the projected aggrandizement of
France be realized, an alteration would be effected in the ſtate of affairs, and in the Balance
of Power, which would expoſe this Country
to the riſk of having hereafter to ſupport a
War againſt that overgrown Republic, without the aſſiſtance or co-operation of any important Ally. In order to eſtimate the probability of this occurrence, we muſt conſider,
that, in the chain of political connexions and
engagements, the Netherlands form the principal, and almoſt the only link, by which this
Country can hold to the great Military Powers
of the Continent. No leſs than England, they
have *all* a *common*, and *ſome* a *ſpecific* intereſt in
the fate of theſe Provinces. To prevent France
from

from acquiring an irrefiftible military afcendancy—to procure a folid and fubftantial Peace
—to preferve the balance of Power, are objects
of general concern to all Europe. The dignity
and permanent interefts of the Houfe of Auftria
are prefling motives for the Emperor not to
relinquifh his right of Sovereignty over this valuable part of his pofleffions. The Empire,
and particularly the Northern parts of Germany, including a confiderable portion of the
Pruffian territories, cannot be in any real ftate
of fecurity, if Holland and the Netherlands are
under the fame power as France. But, on the
fuppofition, that the fovereignty and influence
of France over thefe Countries fhould be eftablifhed, and confirmed by a General Peace,
what relative interefts could exift between this
Country and the King of Hungary? What
mutual advantage and fupport could we then
afford each other? What real grounds of efficient alliance, guarantee, or co-operation, ufeful
to either party, would then remain? Certainly
none. The Emperor might ftill be a great
Power, with refpect to Turkey or Pruffia; but
he could no longer have an influence to exer-
cife, or an inclination to interfere, in the affairs

fairs and altercations of France and England.
Pruffia, at this moment, is, I am afraid, more
difpofed to form a clofe connexion with France
than with this Country : But, even if no engagements fhould exift between them, is it to
be fuppofed that the Court of *Berlin,* or any
of the States of Germany, would form an alliance with England, or offer us their co-operation, whilft the frontier, which feparates
them from a Power infinitely fuperior in the
numbers of its Armies, and every other military advantage, is open on their fide, and defended on the fide of the Enemy by the ftrongeft
works and pofitions of Art and Nature ? With
the example of the prefent War before their
eyes, wonld it not be madnefs for any of them
to engage in hoftilities, which would not even
afford a reafonable chance of preferving a refpectable defenfive pofture ? Nothing but the
moft unprovoked aggreffion could induce them
to take up arms, and even then, perhaps, they
would hefitate between the calamities an unavailing defence would draw on their territories, and the profpect of obtaining better terms
by paffive fubmiffion. We may therefore conclude, that neceffity alone could induce any of
                                             thefe

thefe Powers to take an active part in a conteft
between England and France. But, admitting
the fuppofition, that they were compelled to it
by this or any other motive, the firft confequences of it would certainly be, in fome degree, favourable to us, as a Maritime Power,
inafmuch as it would create a diverfion to the
Naval preparations of the Enemy, divide their
attention and refources, and leave a lefs proportion of men difpofable for the Sea fervice,
or for diftant expeditions. Thefe advantages,
however, would be more than counterbalanced
by the too probable invafion of Germany,
which, if attempted, could hardly fail to fuc-
ceed, at leaft as far as would be neceffary for
cutting off our communication with the rivers
Ems, *Wefer*, and *Elbe*, and thereby depriving
us of all intercourfe with *Hamburgh*, and the
other Ports fituated on thofe rivers, of which
the effect would be more fuddenly and deeply
injurious to our Trade, than that of any other
annoyance it could be expofed to, from the
attempts of the Enemy.

It would be no lefs alarming as a political
event, ifolating us in a manner from Europe;
and, in either point of view, it muft be a matter

ter of anxious confideration to every Englifhman, who has ever turned his thoughts to
commercial or political fubjects—A movement
of the Enemy, of the nature I have fuppofed,
(and to which no real refiftance could be made),
would alfo be attended with the lofs of *Hanover*—a lofs, which, I know, it is much the
fafhion with a certain defcription of perfons to
fpeak of in the flighteft terms, as trifling, and
even defirable for England. It would be foreign
to my purpofe to examine the erroneous and inconfiderate opinions of thofe fuperficial Politi-
cians, as they have been fo often and fuccefsfully
refuted, whenever they have been brought to a
public difcuffion; but I muft requeft of them
to confider the great additional importance the
Electorate would acquire by its near connec-
tion with the Ports and Rivers abovementioned.—As thefe Gentlemen indulge a hope
that *Hanover* may be bartered away in the arrangements of a general Pacification, I muft
add, that any calculation to this effect, whatever advantage may be expected in return, is
unworthy of an Englifhman.—As long as we
recollect that we invited the Sovereigns of that
territory to the Crown of this Country, and
whilft

whilft we gratefully acknowledge the nume-
ous bleffings we have derived from their mild
and beneficent Government, fhall we bafely
abandon the inheritance of their Anceftors ?
No.—The Houfe of *Brunfwick*, in accepting
our invitation, configned the fafety and prefervation of its paternal dominions to the loyal
and generous feelings of Englifhmen, and
Hiftory fhall ever record that we have been
faithful to the truft.

The queftion of the Ceffion of the *Netherlands* might be urged, on the principle of œco-
nomy, as leading to an immediate termination
of the War; but if, reverting to other confiderations already adduced, we reflect how much,
on the one hand, it would curtail our refources,
and, on the other, force us from the preffing
motive of *Security,* to increafe our Peace Eftablifhments, both military and naval, as well
at home as in our foreign poffeffions; we fhall
find that, by a diminution of means, and an
augmentation of expence, the confequence of
faving a few millions at prefent, would be to
expofe ourfelves to lofs of credit, bankruptcy,
and ruin hereafter.

H   It

It has been obferved, that if the *Netherlands* are reftored to the Emperor, he would not be able to retain them, for want of a Barrier of Fortified Towns oppofite to that of France.— I feel the weight of the objection; but it may be overcome in various ways :—If the expence of re-eftablifhing and defending the former line of Fortreffes fhould be found too confiderable; in that event, arrangements might be made between Auftria and Holland, by which the *Meufe*, at leaft, might eafily be rendered a moft refpectable Barrier for the prefervation of Holland, and all the Countries behind that River.—This, I admit, would leave *Brabant* open to the incurfions of the French; but its Sovereignty would not be in danger of being permanently loft.—The policy of Europe muft be, *to oblige France to return within her former limits; to fhew that, whatever extenfion of Territory fhe may fubdue in the courfe of a War, other Powers poffefs fufficient vigour, energy, and refources, not to lay down their Arms, until it fhall be completely reftored.*

This is a great political *maxim*, that ought to be engraved in every State Cabinet of Europe, and to be inalterably impreffed as a *leffon* on the

minds

minds of the Directors of the French Republic. Let this be effected, and Flanders will have a more folid Barrier than all the arts of Engineers can afford, and Europe a better Security for Peace than twenty Treaties, which one or the other Party always makes with a view of break- ing, at fome favourable, and perhaps not diftant, period.

Savoy, the County of *Nice*, and the con- quefts of France on the fide of Italy, are lefs important, in a commercial point of view, than as fubfervient to power, and to farther aggran- dizement. In thefe refpects, every general ar- gument relative to the Netherlands is fully ap- plicabic to thefe acquifitions; the reftoration of which we are, moreover, pledged to obtain by the Third Article of the Treaty between this Country and Sardinia, by which His Ma- jefty engages " not to conclude a Peace with " the Enemy, without comprehending in it " the entire reftitution to His Sardinian Ma- " jefty, of all the parts of his dominions " which belonged to him at the commence- " ment of the War, and of which the Enemy " has obtained poffeffion, or of which it may " hereafter obtain poffeffion during the courfe

" of

" of hoftilities. In return, His Sardinian
" Majefty will continue fi:mly and infeparably
" united and attached to the Common Caufe,
" and to the interefts of His Britannic Ma-
" jefty in this War, not only for fo long a
" time as the War may laft in Italy, or in the
" Southern parts of France, but until the con-
" clufion of Peace between Great Britain and
" France."

Strictly obferving this engagement, and rely-
ing on our good faith, the King of Sardinia
has refufed the Mediation of Spain; and, under
the preffure of the fevereft calamities, continues
faithful to the Common Caufe, with a perfeverance honourable to himfelf, and to the character of Great Britain.

I firmly believe, and fincerely lament, that
the prefent Government of France is refolved
to liften to no Negotiation for the reftoration
either of *Savoy* or the *Netherlands.* With this
difpofition, can we hefitate on the vigorous
prof..ution of the War? Shall the rage of
Aggrandizement be more fuccefsful than the
rage of Subverfion?—Are French Conquefts to
complete the Revolution which French Principles had begun? The Jacobin Club is dif-
perfed,

perfed, but the dregs of it have unfortunately
been raifed to the Directory. In this fupreme
fituation, are they become the Arbiters of the
terms, and the Guardians of the repofe, of
Europe? Have not their Rights of Conqueft
the fame origin as their Rights of Man? The
latter ftrike at the root of Individual, and the
former of National happinefs and tranquillity.
The latter fubvert the principles of private
Property, and eftablifh Anarchy, Equality, and
Violence, on the deftruction of the Laws, Dif-
tinctions, and Reftraints, of civilized Society.
The former fet afide the Laws of Nations, the
Obligations of Treaties, the Sovereignty of
Independent States, and dictate, with the point
of the fword, fuch terms as uncontrouled
Ambition may fuggeft, and paffive Mifery muft
receive, to ftay for a moment the torrent of
Rapine, Plunder, and Carnage.

Born and nurtured amidft thefe fcenes, is it
aftonifhing that the French Republic fhould
trace its origin to the *Rights of Man*, and pretend to derive fupport and folidity from the
Rights of Conqueft?

It is a difpofition natural to every well-dif-
pofed and feeling mind, to be fanguine in the
prefpect

profpect of any event, which muft, in a high degree, conduce to meliorate the fituation of our Fellow-creatures, and to promote the happinefs of our Country. Peace would fo materially contribute to both thefe ends, that the beft-intentioned, though not, perhaps, the moft confiderate men, over anxious to attain this object, are apt to be led aftray by every incoherent fhadow—Let them be on their guard, left, lofing fight of the fubftance, in the eagernefs of their purfuit, they fhould pufh on, regardlefs of other confiderations, until it will be too late to recede; until fenfible of their miftake, but clofely preffed on every fide by the giddy and thoughtlefs multitude, ever ready to follow their illufive wanderings, they can no longer efcape themfelves, or refcue their falling Country from the abyfs of degradation which is open before them. Let them come forward at the prefent critical emergency, and boldly avow their determination to give their affent and fupport to no conditions of Peace, which do not ftipulate the reftitution of all the Conquefts made by France in Europe. —Have they hitherto difcovered any difpofition in the Enemy to negotiate on thefe grounds?

Does

Does not the intelligence of every day bring frefh proofs of the reverfe? To the many I have already adduced, I muft here add one unequivocal and official, which may be found in the following Paper, printed in Englifh at *Paris*.

" A Letter from *London* mentions, that the
" KING, compelled by the wifh of the People,
" has declared to Parliament that he has no
" objection to make Peace with the French
" Republic.

" If the Britifh Miniftry do not deceive
" the People, and their defire for Peace be
" fincere, it will be an eafy matter to con-
" clude it.

" It is held for certain, that our Govern-
" ment, deeply impreffed with the proofs of
" affection held out by the People of England
" towards the French Nation, would infift
" on no other fatisfaction or indemnification,
" *than the refpective reftitution of the French*
" *and Dutch Settlements which are now in the*
" *hands of the Englifh*; and would require
" nothing more of the Britifh Miniftry, *than*
" *that they fhould not interfere with the Internal*
" Government

" *Government of France and Holland, nor in*
" *their War with their Neighbours.*

" The French Government, in professing
" such *amicable dispositions*, only act up to the
" principles they have so often testified, of
" wishing to live in peace and *fraternity* with
" the people of England, indulging the fond
" hope, that a perfect harmony between both
" Nations would conduce to the happiness of
" all Mankind."

This arrogant Declaration, it may be observed, has long been published.—I know it;
but until it appeared by the letter from Citizen *Fonfenberte*, the French National Commis-
sioner in *Holland*, to Citizen *Beiffelier*, *Chargé
d'Affaires* of the Republic at *Bremen*, and
from other channels of information, that it
was prepared by the French Government, and
circulated by the Ministers of the Republic
in foreign residences, I could only consider it
as the unmeaning insolence of a *Jacobin* News-
paper, and not in the light I now do, as an
official Answer to the King's Message, since
it is the only Paper in which His Majesty's
pacific disposition has been expressly noticed.

The

The Emperor and the Empire, we are af-
fured, are refolved to liften to no Negotiation,
but on the principles of the *Status quo ante
Bellum* ; whilft, on the other hand, the Directory, and all it's fubordinate Agents, take every
opportunity of declaring, that the *Auſtrian Netherlands* are fo irrecoverably acquired to France,
as not even to be made the fubject matter of
Negotiation.—To which of thefe principles is
Great Britain to fubfcribe ?—On the iſſue of
this great queſtion depends the Pacification of
Europe.

Having fairly ſtated the only terms, with
refpect to the Continent of Europe, on which
a fubſtantial and honourable Peace can be concluded, and the difficulties by which it is likely
to be retarded, I ſhall proceed briefly to in-
veſtigate the relative fituations of England,
France, and Holland, in the Eaſt and Weſt
Indies, (including in the former the *Cape of
Good Hope*) with a view to the fame refults.

Having reduced all the French Settlements
on the Continent of *Aſia*, and maſters as we
are of the *Cape* and *Trincomale*, with a fuperior
Naval Force, I may fairly aſſume, that ſhould
the prefent War be protracted, we ſhall remain

I   invulnerable

invulnerable in that quarter, and that, whatever is recovered to the Enemy of our prefent
Conquefts, or of thofe we may hereafter make,
muft be fo by the refult of Negotiation.——
This being the cafe, it will only be neceffary
to confider the fituation of our Indian Empire,
and to compare the objects we have in view in
that quarter, with the claims and pretenfions of
the French and Dutch, in order diftinctly to
draw the line between what may eventually
be reftored, in return for conceffions of equal
importance in Europe, (if they cannot otherwife be obtained) and what can never be given
up, without facrificing or endangering the deareft interefts and concerns of this Country.

The nature of the Englifh Empire in India
being generally known, I fhall confine myfelf
to remark, that the undifturbed and fecure en-
joyment of the *Sovereignty* we have acquired
over thofe immenfe and valuable Provinces,
muft be our firft object, to which even our
Commerce becomes a fecondary confideration ;
As long as we can preferve the former, there
cannot be a doubt but the latter will continue
gradually improving and increafing : But fhould
our *Sovereignty* be loft, not only the greateft

part

part of our Commerce, but the numerous other channels through which India contributes to the profperity and grandeur of this Country, would be annihilated; and it might then be truly faid, that the *Sun of Great Britain was fet for ever.* To watch every opportunity, and to feize every means of adding to the folidity and ftability of our Indian Empire, is therefore unqueftionably the firft confideration for the Britifh Government in that quarter of the world; and with this view, it is their indifpenfible duty to place it, as far as human forefight can effect, out of the reach of any rival European Power. Whoever admits thefe premifes, muft, at the fame time, admit, that the Settlement of the *Cape* is the moft important acquifition which could be made by Great Britain. From it's fituation, it may truly be called the key of India. No European Power can entertain a reafonable expectation of fending to that diftant part of the world an Expedition fufficiently formidable to threaten the fafety of our Eftablifhments there, unlefs it fhould be previoufly poffeffed of the facility of refitting and obtaining refrefhments at fome intermediate point on it's paffage.

No

No Power, in actual hostility with Great Britain, can enjoy this advantage, as long as we shall retain the *Cape* and *St. Helena*; and although a Fleet might reach India without touching at either of these possessions, it would be so disabled and unfit for active operations, as, almost to a certainty, to allow us the time necessary for taking such steps as might render the intentions for which it was sent unattainable, before any effort could be made for carrying them into execution.—By the addition of the *Cape* and *Trincomalé* to our present establishments, it appears to me, that we should possess every requisite that prudence can suggest, as necessary to the permanent safety, tranquillity, and prosperity of our Eastern Territories.

It may be asked, whether, in the event of a favourable turn of affairs in Europe, under which the United Provinces might again become our Ally, it would not be just and politic to relinquish an arrangement which tends to deprive them of these valuable Settlements?—My answer is, that whenever the Netherlands shall be recovered, either by the result of Negotiation, or by the progress of the Austrian Arms,

Arms, the Dutch will then be liberated from
the tyrannic yoke of the French, and, ceafing
to become our Enemies, may, in the courfe of
political events, renew their union and friend-
fhip with this Country.—But let us fuppofe
this happy change of affairs actually to have
taken place, I have no hefitation to fay, that
even under that contingency, the intereft of
the United Provinces, well underftood, would
induce them to cede the *Cape* and *Trincomalé*
to England.

The connections of Holland in the Eaft
Indies are, and muft be, confined to commercial purfuits. She has neither the means to
acquire, nor to preferve an Empire. Every
eftablifhment which has not for its object to
improve or protect her trade, is an unneceffary
and ruinous expence. Such were the *Cape* and
Trincomalé to the Dutch Eaft India Company.
No valuable part of their trade with India was
immediately derived from thofe Settlements,
which, from their nature and fituation, are
highly fubfervient to power and protection,
and in no refpect conducive to the extenfion of
commercial enterprize. They will at all times
be rather a burden, than a direct fource of re-
venue

venue, to the State which may poffefs them; and if this confideration was not over-ruled by others of greater weight, it might be rather defirable than otherwife, that thefe Conquefts fhould be replaced under the dominion of Holland, as foon as our alliance with that Country could be re-eftablifhed; but, in that cafe, the Dutch would not be poffeffed of fufficient means to render them fecure.

France is the only State whofe rivality and power can be dangerous to us in the Eaft. As long as Holland fhall remain under her dominion, or even her Ally, our own fafety requires that thefe important Pofts fhould be in our Poffeffion, in order that the advantages they afford may not be turned againft us; and whenever Holland fhall enter into friendly engagements with us, and will thereby be more or lefs expofed to follow our fortunes in the event of a rupture with France, the fafety and protection of her own poffeffions in the Eaft will require that the *Cape* and *Trincomalé*, as the great bulwarks of the whole, fhould be under the dominion of Great Britain, becaufe it is not in the power of the Dutch Government

to

to fupply them with proper Garrifons, and other adequate means of defence.

In fhort, the diftant Poffeffions of Holland cannot ftand by themfelves. They muft owe their fecurity to the affiftance either of France or England. If France be her Ally, a due attention to our own prefervation forbids us to part with the *Cape* and *Trincomalé*. If England be her Ally, thefe poffeffions, in our Hands, will afford an efficient protection, inftead of occafioning any detriment or diminution to her Trade, and, to our mutual advantage, will enable us fuccefsfully to oppofe any hoftile efforts of the common Enemy in that part of the World.

The infignificant defence made by the *Cape* and *Trincomalé*, are ftrong proofs that the Dutch, unaffifted, are incapable of maintaining a conteft in the Eaft with France or England; and, indeed, I cannot advert to this circumftance, to the general belief which prevailed in Europe of the weak and unprovided ftate of thefe Settlements, and to the no lefs general knowledge of the vaft advantage an active and powerful Enemy might derive from them in a conteft with us, without feeling greatly aftonifhed that,

not

not only they never attracted the notice of the French during the two years of the present War, during which Holland was engaged in the Coalition as our Ally, but that no precaution appears to have been taken to prevent their falling into our hands, when the Invasion of Holland obliged us to undertake their reduction.

I cannot mention this unaccountable instance of supineness or ignorance on the part of an Enemy, whose operations, in general, have been ably concerted and skilfully conducted, without noticing, at the same time, the active and provident measures of Administration, and congratulating my Country on their happy results.

It is highly probable that *Batavia, Malacca, Cochin, Amboyna*, and nearly all the other Dutch Settlements in India, are before this time reduced under the British dominion. It is a question of too much delicacy for me to discuss, whether it will be politic and necessary to restore them all to the Dutch, and to give back *Pondicherry* and the French Factories to France. The arrangements, in this respect, will depend very much on the circumstances of the War,

and

and many political events which may occur before any Negotiation can be entered upon and concluded. Should their reftitution be neceffary, and compenfated by equivalent advantages, obtained to ourfelves or our Allies in fome other quarter, I conceive they may be reftored, and even, according to circumftances, rendered of more weight in the fcale of Negotiation by liberal commercial arrangements, without difgrace, or real danger to the leading, fubftantial, and permanent interefts of this Country in India; but this, however, is a point on which I by no means pretend to give a pofitive opinion—but I do moft pofitively affirm, that no arrangement ought to be admitted by this Country, which does not leave us in poffeffion of the *Cape* and *Trincomalé*. They will add nothing to the refources of the powerful Empire we poffefs, but infinitely to its fecurity.— The Enemy, on the contrary, having no Sovereignty to preferve in India, can only value them as inftruments to undermine and deftroy ours.

Should they be put in poffeffion of thefe advantages, their future attempts might and would probably fail of fuccefs; but why place the

K   weapons

weapons in their hands, and thereby invite them to the attack ?

The cafe of abfolute neceffity is the only juftifiable anfwer can be given to this queftion, and it is the only confideration to which the fpirit of the Country fhould fubmit when points of fuch magnitude are at ftake.

The difcuffion of future arrangements in the Eaft Indies, arifing out of the prefent circumftances of the War, is rendered clear and precife by the great diftinction exifting between the interefts, and the relative fituations of this Country, and of the Enemy, in that quarter.— I cannot allow myfelf to fuppofe, that Adminiftration is not fully aware of the leading principles by which my obfervations have been guided, or that they will for a moment lofe fight of them, whenever they fhall become the fubject of Negotiation.—With this fatisfactory impreffion on my mind, I could wifh to terminate this inveftigation ; but the nature of it obliges to meet the more arduous tafk of hazarding a few obfervations on the State of the War, and of the expectations this Country may form with refpect to the Weft Indies.

In

In this quarter the conduct of the French
has been directed, not to useful conquests, but
to devastation—Here they have been unremit-
tingly and too succesfully employed in schemes
of destruction—Here they have established a
Policy and Government, founded upon principles incompatible with the safety and tranquillity of adjoining Colonies; principles which,
in the opinion of every man acquainted with
the European Settlements in the West Indies,
must, in the course of a few years, infallibly
lead to their total subverfion, unless the French
can be compelled by force, or induced by negotiation to relinquish those Principles, and
to place the poffeflions they may retain under
regulations of a similar tendency and effect
with those, which prevail in the Colonies of
other Powers, instead of industriously persisting
in their present plans of spreading immediate,
unconditional emancipation, equality, and revolt
through all the islands, which have hitherto
flourished under a system so directly opposite.
My object here is to state facts, and not to
examine the question of the Slave Trade or the
Slave Laws.—Considering them as outrages on
human nature, I sincerely hope that, when the

present

present ferment shall have subsided, the wisdom of the Legislature will devise some means of gradually abolishing these evils; but certainly the most prejudiced opponent of the barbarous practice I now condemn will admit, that the revolutionary expedients by which the French restore slaves to freedom are more to be apprehended at this moment, and pregnant with greater prospective calamities, than can possibly arise from the continuance of this unnatural power over our fellow creatures.

This circumstance of the Enemy's behaviour is a most serious obstacle to the possibility of any satisfactory arrangement with respect to the West Indies.—The first difficulty, in that quarter, will not be to settle a line of demarcation, and to determine between what conquests *may* be restored, and what *must* be retained, but to eradicate destructive principles, and to prevent proceedings, which, from their dangerous tendency, and contaminating example, cannot be continued under the sanction and countenance of the French Government, even with the islands subject to their sovereignty, without exposing those of other Powers to the same ruinous consequences.

It

It is impofiible to confider the prefent period
of the War, the unparalleled misfortunes of
our Weft India expeditions, the immenfe Britifh property involved in Weft India fpeculations, the actual ftate of our iflands, and the
apparently defperate refolution of the Enemy
not to depart from their abominable purfuits,
without feeling the moft alarming concern.—
We muft not deceive ourfelves as to the extent
of the object, or of the danger. It is by a juft
knowledge of the one, and a full fenfe of the
other, that we may hope fuccefsfully to meet
by far the greateft difficulties which contribute
to retard a Pacification.

The truly calamitous outfet of the Weft
India Expedition, arifing from a feries of un-
toward events, which no human Power could
forefee or controul, has confiderably dimi-
nifhed the profpect of advantages, which, under
lefs adverfe circumftances, might reafonably
have been expected from the enfuing campaign.—Our fituation and advantages, however, may ftill be materially ameliorated and
improved before the feafon for active operations
is over, fhould the weather ceafe to baffle our
efforts, and allow our gallant Troops and their
fkilful

skilful Commanders to exert againſt the common Enemy the ſame admirable zeal and ſpirit,
as have induced them to perſevere in their
laudable attempt to reſiſt and ſubdue the un-
governable rage of the elements. In the preſent poſture of affairs, I frankly own that it
appears to me impoſſible to ſuggeſt any arrangement likely to lead to a ſatisfactory and
ſafe reſult.—After the moſt minute and anxious
conſideration, no expedient immediately practicable has occurred to me, which is not re-
plete with the moſt imminent danger. Until
the iſſue of the Campaign ſhall be known, he
muſt be a bold, and even a raſh man, who will
take upon himſelf the Reſponſibility of re-
ſtoring Peace to the Weſt Indies, upon terms
conſiſtent with their future preſervation and
ſecurity.—The only aſſiſtance I can preſume
to offer is, to point out the numerous rocks
on which he may ſplit; but it muſt be his
own buſineſs to erect the beacons which may
ſerve to guide the veſſel into a ſafe port.

In the Leeward Iſlands, *Guadaloupe* and *St.*
Lucia are occupied by a horde of *Banditti*,
who can hardly be ſaid to be completely under
the Government of the French Republic; and
this

this circumstance, in fact, renders them more dangerous, as it leaves less hope of an amelioration in the posture of affairs, in case a pacific system, or any other favourable occurrence arising in France; should induce her to discountenance their barbarous proceedings; to which, however, she appears firmly resolved to give her most strenuous assistance and support.

This odious disposition of the French Government may be collected from the Article of their new Constitution, granting *Liberty* and *Equality* to the Negroes ; from the sentiments manifested in the Message of the Directory on the subject of the Colonies; and the Proclamation General *Lavaux* has lately published at *St. Domingo,* in conformity, no doubt, to their instructions.

These public Acts are so many unequivocal proofs of their firm resolution to establish *Liberty, Equality,* and *Fraternity* in the West Indies.—In conformity to the solemn pledge of their disposition in this respect given, to the Negroes by the new Constitution, *Lavaux* emphatically calls upon *Citizens of all Colours,* " to enjoy these inestimable Benefits, to follow " the Example of their Brethren in France,

" to

" to fhare in their fuccefies, and to confider
" themfelves all as Children of the fame Re-
" public, which has declared the Colonies
" integral parts of it's forces, and that nothing
" could diffolve her Indivifibility."

Thefe Declarations, and the preparations
made in France for enabling *Lavaux, Victor
Hugues,* and their Affociates, to execute their
further plans of Devaftation, leave no hope
that the Enemy will retract, or voluntarily
crufh the principles, which threaten deftruction to the Weft Indies—They have already
reached and laid wafte two of our valuable
Iflands, and feveral others are under the daily
apprehenfion of the fame calamities.

Forming my judgment from experience, the
communications of the moft intelligent Mer-
chants and Planters, and the opinions of Naval
and Military Characters, well acquainted with
the Leeward Iflands, I feel impreffed with a
conviction, that there can be no real and permanent fecurity for our poffeffions or trade
in that quarter, until *Guadaloupe* and *St. Lucia*
fhall be wrefted from the hands of the Enemy;
or until the Affociation, at prefent prevailing
in thofe Iflands, of Revolutionary Affafins,
Pirates,

Pirates, and Plunderers of every defcription, fhall be fuperfeded by fome regular fyftem of interior policy, poffeffed of authority to enforce the obfervance of the general laws of civilized nations, and of the local ufages and practices applicable to the peculiar nature of the Weft India Colonies; and equally obferved by all, as neceffary to their exiftence and prefervation. I have procured the opinions of many perfons fuppofed to be moft competent to decide on the accuracy of this alarming obfervation, and every one has uniformly concurred in every part of it. *Martinique* unqueftionably is a military Poft of the greateft importance, and, as fuch, may provide for it's own fafety, but unfortunately we have fufficient proof that it cannot afford an adequate protection to all the Britifh Iflands of the *Charibbean* Sea, againft the Enemy at prefent occupying *Guadaloupe* and *St. Lucia.*—The fituation of thefe two laft Iflands is particularly conducive and favourable to the fuccefs of their prefent Warfare; and the latter is, moreover, poffeffed of an Harbour, which adds greatly to the importance of it's fituation.—*Martinique,* however, as a productive and well-cultivated Colony, is a

L   valuable

valuable acquisition, and, as a Fortress, of the
utmost consequence; but we must not forget
that it's strong works are an unavailing barrier
against revolutionary measures.—A complete
change of disposition in the Enemy, or their
total expulsion, can alone prevent the continuance of these calamities.—The execution
of this last mentioned enterprize, should it be
undertaken, will be materially affifted by the
poffeffion of *Martinique*—Had it been in the
hands of the French, the difafters, at prefent
confined to *Grenada* and *St. Vincent's*, would
inevitably have been extended to all our Settlements—As long as *Martinique* fhall remain a
Britifh Colony, it will give us a facility for
recovering any of our former poffeffions, which
the Enemy, in their predatory incurfions,
may have entirely, or in part, reduced under
their dominion.—On the fuppofition that, with
the return of Peace, the French, from neceffity, intereft, or inclination, fhould renounce
their deftructive proceedings; and that, in the
event of a future rupture, their operations in
the Weft Indies would be conducted upon the
principles adopted by civilized nations, *Martinique* becomes an object of the utmoft confequence

fequence to this Country, either with a view
to offenfive meafures, or for the eftablifhment
of a folid fyftem of defence. If *Guadaloupe*
and *St. Lucia* cannot be reconquered and pre-
ferved, it would be the only point in that *Ar-
chipelago*, capable of fuch refiftance, as might
afford us time, either to come to it's relief, or
to put our other Colonies in a refpectable ftate
of defence.

The natural inferences to be drawn from
this ftatement are, that to reftore *Martinique*
to the French would be virtually to give up to
them all our *Charibbee* Iflands.—That the poffeffion of this Colony, without *Guadaloupe*
and *St. Lucia*, might afford a reafonable degree
of fecurity to the Britifh Settlements, if the
operations of the Enemy fhould be directed to
views of ufeful conqueft, inftead of favage
devaftation—That fhould they, as appears probable, perfift in this laft mode of Warfare,
there can be no alternative between the reduction of the two Iflands from which it is carried
on, and the imminent rifk of feeing it gradually extended to all our poffeffions, and fucceffively involving them in fubverfion, plunder,
and ruin.

L 2

In

In *Jamaica* we have the fame dangers to guard againſt from *St. Domingo*, as in the Charibbee Iſlands from *Guadaloupe* and *St. Lucia* —This moſt valuable Colony, by the protection it derives from *Cape Nicolas Mole*, from our ſuperior Naval Force, and it's own means of Defence, may be conſidered as perfectly ſecure againſt any hoſtile attempt the Enemy could make, during the preſent War, with a view to it's reduction ; but if, at the Peace, we ſhould abandon to the French our Poſts in *St. Domingo*, and ſhould ſuffer them to retain the *Spaniſh*, in addition to their former poſſeſſions in that Iſland, the ſituation of *Jamaica* would then become extremely precarious and inſecure. Should the French be able and willing to re-eſtabliſh Order and good Government in *St. Domingo*, *Jamaica*, I admit, would have nothing to apprehend, as long as Peace and good Underſtanding could be preſerved between France and England ; but at the renewal of hoſtilities, it is not improbable that the loſs of that Colony might be the firſt reſult of a Pacification, by which the French would be reinſtated in the Poſts at preſent

occupied

occupied by the Britifh at *St. Domingo*, and allowe] the undifturbed poffeffion of the *Spanifh* part of the Ifland.—Such were probably their views and pretenfions in concluding a Peace with Spain, in which the interefts of this Country were certainly not confulted.

How far this conceffion may be found an obftacle to the Ceffation of Hoftilities, I cannot pretend to determine; but the dignity and intereft of this Country certainly require that that we fhould not inconfiderately give up Ports of fuch vaft importance as *Cape Nicolas Mole*, become a party to this violation of the Treaty of *Utrecht*, and fubmit to an arrangement which would give the French a decided and dangerous fuperiority in that quarter.

I will not anticipate the confequences of a Treaty, which, without impofing any reftraint on the revolutionary proceedings of the French in *St. Domingo*, would leave them the entire fovereignty of that Ifland; becaufe, I truft, no man will prefume fo far to difregard the experience of recent calamities, and the juft apprehenfions of our own Settlements, as to purchafe Peace on fuch terms, unlefs he fhall

be

be really compelled to it, by the moft dif-
aftrous and hitherto unforefeen events.

I have not adverted to the immenfe advantages England would derive from the poffeffion of *St. Domingo*; becaufe, in inveftigating
our Weft India interefts with a reference to the
exifting profpects of Peace, I have confined my
enquiry to the apparent pofture of affairs at
the prefent moment—It is fuch, in my opinion, as affords neither the means of advantageous Negotiation, nor of permanent Security; but the Campaign is not yet fo far ad-
vanced, or the ftate of our Expeditions fo
defperate, as to preclude a reafonable hope of
acquiring, in the courfe of this year, both
thofe defirable objects, and of rendering the
Weft Indies no lefs fubfervient than the Eaft,
to the attainment of an honourable and advantageous Peace for ourfelves, and our Allies in
Europe, and to the future grandeur and profperity of this Country.

I have hitherto remained filent on the fubject
of *Corfica*; becaufe I freely confefs I am not
fufficiently acquainted with the circumftances
and importance of this Acquifition, to be prepared to give any opinion on the fubject.—If
it

it affords us an advantageous port in the Mediterranean, an influence with the Powers, and a beneficial participation in the trade of the Levant and Italy, and, if from His Majefty's acceptance of the *Corfican* Crown, it cannot be reftored without difgrace, I hope the intereft and honour of Great Britain will determine His Majefty's Minifters to infift on the prefervation of that ifland, as one of the conditions of peace. On the other hand, fhould its importance in the fcale of negotiation be eftimated by the latter confideration only, I truft that fome expedient will be fuggefted for conciliating the dignity of Great Britain with the neceffity of terminating as foon as poffible the calamities of War.

I cannot conclude thefe obfervations without noticing an article in the Official Journal of the French Directory, in which, fpeaking of their political fituation, an intimation is given of the probability of a counter-alliance being oppofed to the exifting Coalition of England and the two Imperial Courts. The words are, " *A l'exterieur, une Guerre qui menace* " *le Nord de l'Europe; une contre-alliance qui* " *peut-*

" *peut-être fous peu f'ra oppofée à la Coalition*
" *que ous avons à cem at're.*"

The expectation of fuch an occurrence may
perhaps fupport the hopes and infolent pretenfions of the Directory ; but if *Sweden* fhould become fo entirely the venal inftrument of
France, if *Pruffia* fhould be inclined to facrifice her dignity, the conftitutional integrity of
the Empire, and her own permanent interefts,
to the unworthy motive of thwarting and op-
pofing the plans and juft expectations of the
Emperor, or to the illufive promifes of France.
—If Spain, from the influence of French
councils, or other ill-judged motives, fhould
alfo give affiftance to this unnatural and mon-
ftrous Alliance, it may contribute to protract
and extend the calamities of War, but not to
compel *England*, *Auftria*, and *Ruffia*, to ignominious fubmiffion. Europe may then be-
hold with aftonifhment the Chiefs of the Houfe
of *Bourbon*, and the Family of Orange, wan-
dering in exile, whilft the ufurped govern-
ments of their Affaffins and Perfecutors receive
aid and fupport from the *Spanifh* and *Pruffian*
Monarchies,

Whatever

Whatever motives the French Government may have for refufing to acquiefce in the univerfal anxiety for Peace, it is fome confolation for us, in looking forward to the inevitable continuance of the War, to indulge a reafonable expectation, that, in the courfe of the enfuing campaign, the fituation of England and of its Allies will be improved, and the means of negotiation encreafed.—The late rapid fuc-ceffes of the Auftrians—their vigorous preparations for opening the campaign—the effectual affiftance which the final adjuftment of the partition of *Poland* may enable Ruffia to afford—the favorable intelligence expected from the Eaft Indies—the probability of fome effectual efforts being ftill made in the Weft—the embarraffed fituation of the Enemy—the fpirit of defertion prevalent in their armies, and of difcontent in the interiour.—All thefe circumftances continue to juftify the profpect of a rapid amelioration in our relative fituations, which may lead to a more fpeedy and fatisfactory arrangement than any premature propofals, which the Enemy, in their prefent difpofition, would confider as proofs of weaknefs, approaching to fubmiffion.

M

I will

. I will not calculate the probability of obtaining better terms than thofe I have now fuggefted, or the chance of favourable Revolutions which might arife from great but not impoffible events, in the prefent ftate of France, (fuch as the triumph cf the Royalift, or Moderate Party) as motives for continuing the War; but I mention them as confiderations not entirely to be difregarded under the impoffibility of a Peace.

I have now ftated the terms from which I conceive we cannot depart without rifking our own fecurity—the protection we owe to our commerce and diftant poffeffions—without breaking our engagements with our Allies, and thereby forfeiting our afcendancy in Europe, the dignity and character of the nation, and every advantage derived from internal happinefs and foreign confideration.

The Statefman whofe good fortune it may be to reftore the bleffings of Peace on thefe terms, will not feel a more fincere joy than I fhall, in the attainment of this happy event— Here will begin the contraft between the effects of a provident Adminiftration, bringing a moft difficult conteft to a happy iffue

by

by the ordinary refources of induftry and freedom, by the perfevering fupport of a fpirited People, by the regular fupplies of Credit ;—and the deftructive power of a Revolutionary Government, obtaining by confifcation and terror what confidence and public fpirit could not fupply, and making the lives, the liberty, and the poffeffions of every individual the fport of its caprices, or the inftruments of its ambition.—To augment individual and thereby add to public Profperity, to extend our Commerce, to improve our Induftry, to reduce our National Debt, to raife our Credit—fuch will be the eafy and pleafing cares of the Britifh Adminiftration ; whilft that of France will have the wide extended fcene of private and national Diftrefs, Bankruptcy, Stagnation of Trade, Deftruction of Induftry and Capitals, conftantly before its eyes, without the means of miniftring relief to the wants of its fuffering fubjects, or providing for the expences of the State. The wretched and divided Citizens of France will then attempt, by heterogeneous attributes and unavailing props, to give confiftency and fupport to the tottering monument of their Con-

ftitution,

ftitution, raifed by the hands of Regicides, and cemented by the blood of Innocence; while Englifhmen will emulate with each other in ftrengthening that venerable Fabric from which our happinefs is derived—More than a century has now elapfed fince one fhort ftorm fwept from around its pillars the laft corroding vapours of aefpotic Power; but in France the moft violent hurricanes follow each other in rapid fucceffion, and inftead. of purifying its lefs fortunate atmofphere, appear only to engender frefh clouds of mifery and oppreffion.

May England thus be an example, and France a warning to Europe!

February 2, 1796.

POSTSCRIPT.

THE obfervations I have prefumed to offer to the Public, on the difpofition of the Enemy, were fent to the Prefs before the Intelligence of the important and extraordinary Meffage which appears to have been fent by the French Directory to the Council of Antients, on the 24th of January, had reached this Country.

In calling upon my Readers to remark the exact Coincidence of the Sentiments and Views, emphatically announced in this Meffage, with the Difpofitions I have afcribed to the reftlefs and ambitious Governors of the French Republic, I am not afraid that they will fufpect me of obtruding upon their patience for the unworthy purpofe of deriving credit from the obfervation.—On the contrary, without a reference to my former opinions, my exultation at the approach to Peace would have been as truly fincere as my regret is now deeply felt at the increafed Profpect of the continuance of the War. This Meffage cannot fail to excite the attention of Parliament, in the interefting Debate which will probably take place on Mr. *Grey*'s intended Motion for Peace.—I do

not

not pretend to anticipate the Obfervations and Declarations to which it may give rife, and much lefs to fcrutinize the Secrets of State, or to dive into the Myfteries of the Cabinet ; but, I own, I fhall be much aftonifhed if it fhould appear that the Directory has, agreeably to its affertion, offered any fpecific Terms of Peace to the Coalefced Powers.—Perhaps this affertion alludes to the anfwer given to the Emperor's Propofal, made through the Court of *Denmark*—to the Decrees by which *Savoy* and the *Netherlands* are united to France—to the conftitutional Article which enumerates all their former Colonies as integral Parts of the Republic, *One* and *Indivifible* ;—to their arrogant Declaration on the fubject of the King's Meffage.—Or more probably to all thefe feparate pretenfions, comprized under the general defcription of " *Conditions as moderate as the National Dignity will admit of.*"

Is it for thefe Conditions that another Campaign is to be undertaken ?—that the Directory calls upon it's devoted flaves to return to the " *blood-ftained Plains of War ?*"

If no other terms have been offered, it is natural to imply that fuch are their pretenfions. They leave us no alternative. The certainty

of

of an unfuccefsful Campaign would be pre-
ferable to immediate fubmiffion on fuch
Terms.—Perfeverance, even under Defeat, by
exhaufting the laft inadequate refources of the
Enemy, would render Moderation neceffary.—
It is not, however, this perfeverance that will
be required; on the contrary, the fituation of
affairs affords a reafonable expectation that the
events of the enfuing Campaign will enable us
to accomplifh our irrevocable refolution, to
reftore the Balance of Power; to remain faithful to our engagements; to fupport the National Character; to do juftice to the prefent,
and to difcharge our Duty to all future, Generations.

As I have no other object than to point out
the Sentiments of the French Directory with
refpect to Peace, I fhall not enter into a further
examination of this Meffage; but I cannot help
noticing their avowal that the Republic is *not*
" *poffeffed of any reprefentative Signs of Exchange.*"
What is become of *Thirty Milliards* of *Affignats?*
Were they not mortgaged upon all the National
Domains which they reprefented? Has not a
Paper Currency, unlimited in it's amount,
been hitherto the medium of all exchanges,
and the fource of all the terrific Power of
France?

France ?—Six Months ago it was their boaſt, that their pecuniary reſources were ſuperior to thoſe of all Europe ; and now they complain of the *total Abſence of the repreſentative Signs of Exchange !*—They have at laſt learned by experience, that Money can only be the common medium of exchange, by being the common meaſure of all exchangeable Articles. All other Repreſentatives, not poſſeſſed of an intrinſic Value, come under the deſcription of *Credit*, and can only be permanently ſupported by a confidence in the uninterrupted facility of exchanging them for the real Value for which they are iſſued and received. After the avowal of this Meſſage, who can doubt that the reſource of the Aſſignats is annihilated ? This Alteration in the State of their Affairs will lead more rapidly to a ſafe and honourable Peace than all the Auſtrian Victories on the Rhine, of which it is perhaps a principal pre-diſpoſing cauſe, requiring, in it's turn, to be aided and accelerated by the ſpeedy opening of another Campaign, which will prove, I truſt, as brilliant, as the Concluſion of the laſt.

February 5, 1796.

www.ingramcontent.com/pod-product-compliance
Lightning Source LLC
Chambersburg PA
CBHW032251080426
42735CB00008B/1086